1001 Decorating Ideas

Dens & Family Rooms

Galahad Books • New York City

Contents

Introduction

Every family needs a room where they can relax and pursue their hobbies or studies away from the formal parts of the house. In many cases, a basement or attic can be easily turned into a family room — an area for game-playing, television-viewing, and family gatherings. A spare bedroom can be used as a den or sewing room most of the time, as a guest room when company visits. And a garden room, filled with plants and easy-care furnishings, is perfect for informal entertaining and family gatherings.

The important thing to remember when furnishing a family room or den is that it should encourage informality. The furniture upholstery should be stain-resistant, the flooring resilient. If the den doubles as a guest room, there should be a comfortable bed or sleep sofa and a place for visitors to store belongings. If the room is used as an office or hobby area, good lighting should be a priority.

On the following pages, you'll find ideas for turning basements, lofts, spare bedrooms, and even extra-large closets into areas the entire family can enjoy.

Many thanks to 1001 Decorating Ideas.

Chapter 1
Family Rooms

Today's family rooms are home entertainment centers. Besides the TV set, they are furnished with game tables, stereo equipment, and a piano or organ. Nor is the family room for family use only. It's the perfect place for the bridge or garden club to meet, for a birthday party, or for a Sunday brunch.

A former kitchen window now serves as a pass-through to this family room; shutters close to hide the kitchen. Beside the bar, a sturdy étagère stores glasses. On the opposite side of the room, an octagonal glass-topped table with upholstered lounge chairs is handy for games, snacks, and hobbies. Speakers for the stereo are inconspicuously mounted in the ceiling. Bright orange and chrome spice up the neutral color scheme.

Photos: Darwin Davidson/Design: Frederick Twist

8

Antique beams and barn siding are a foil for "poster palette" colors in this family room. The brilliantly patterned window shade and ceiling colors are echoed in the sofa patterns, molded vinyl chairs and table, and painted captain's chair. A modern hooded fireplace coexists compatibly with an antique "gunpowder" cabinet.

S tenciling is used to decorate this family room. Walls and love seats are covered in a stencil-look pattern. A paint-it-yourself stencil plays up the table, chairs, and the window shades; the pattern is based on a motif from the wall covering. An antique Delft tile design is reproduced in the easy-care vinyl flooring. Antique blue wall units provide storage and two desks.

Photo: Ernie Silva/Design: Patricia Hart McMillan

Photo: Vince Lisanti

The game room in Mike Douglas' house was a staff dining room and sitting room before the dividing wall was torn down. Its focal point, of course, is the big billiards table beneath a Tiffany-style chandelier. There are tables for chess and other games. Behind the tall director's chair, a memento from "The Carol Burnett Show," is a photo montage done by one of his fans.

12

This A-frame home's family room is attractive and comfortable. And it's easy to afford: it is designed with few furnishings and plenty of floor coverings. A series of platforms covered with carpeting over carpet cushion provide seating. Throw pillows, built-ins, and yards of carpeting in warm, earthy tones complete the look.

Design: Edmund Motyka, ASID

Dark beams and timbers, a stained-glass window, and a gateleg table recall 17th-century England in this family room. The carpeting echoes the window's stained-glass effect, adds country charm, and — when stapled to the wall — "soundproofs" the niche holding the television. An oak Windsor chair and butler's tray table face a contemporary sofa covered in a patchwork-pattern fabric.

Photo: Ernie Silva/Design: Patricia Hart McMillan

Great for work and play, this room boasts an office, family area with seating center, and game area. An L-shaped sectional sofa sets the bounds of the conversation area. Easily moved bunching tables are a clue that one of the sofa's sections becomes a queen-sized bed. The focal point of this area is a freestanding fireplace, ensconced in a brick-lined corner on a raised hearth. The custom-designed desk has a hinged upper level that extends the width of the desk and opens to reveal suspended file folders. The extended work surface is also a hinged drawing board. Behind the desk, panel folding doors of stained ponderosa pine conceal closets and tall file cabinets. Lined draperies draw for nighttime warmth.

Photos: Vince Lisanti/Design: Evan Frances, ASID

Warm wood paneling, "nostalgic" oak furniture, easy-care upholstery, and Colonial red carpeting transform a once-formidable, formal dining room into this comfortable family/dining room. Paneling covers cracked and crooked walls; its rich wood color and slightly distressed finish add just the right amount of warmth and coziness. A pass-through to the kitchen, fitted with a convenient serving counter, is a step-saving device. Louvered shutters can close off the view of the kitchen. In order to leave ample floor space for two love seats as well as for the dining table and chairs, the buffet is built into a niche. An open shelf above the buffet holds cups and saucers. Behind the shelf, the wall is mirrored to expand the room visually and to add "pizazz." An old-fashioned stained-glass window adds color. The niche surrounding the window is filled in with bookshelves. A shelf across the top of the window holds a collection of plates, and a platform behind the baseboard heating elements becomes a convenient spot for plants.

Photos: Alan Hicks/Design: Russell English & Mark Perry

Here is another view of the family room
shown on the previous page. You can see the
louvered doors that close off the view into the
kitchen.

Visual space is expanded in this family room
by using a large photomural of a New England
landscape. The reproduction "horse" weather-
vane adds drama and, with the American flag
picture and salt box on the wall, keynotes the
early American theme. Rattan trunks do double
duty as tables and provide storage for family-
centered hobbies and games. French doors give
easy access to the outside deck. A game table
with turn-over top for either checkers or back-
gammon awaits a friendly bout.

Photos: Bill Hedrich/Design: Patricia Laughman & J. Christopher Jones

A carefree place for friendly gatherings, this hearth-centered family room is ready for holiday entertaining. The L-shaped modular seating in a rugged, easy-care fabric is angled to take best advantage of the fireplace. A rich navy carries the color load in this room and is a striking contrast to the neutrals of the rustic wood-paneled walls and beamed ceiling. Glass medallions with a Yuletide theme decorate the window. The baker's rack has a wood cabinet base large enough to stash the television.

Photo: Vince Lisanti

This library, belonging to opera star Roberta Peters, was enlarged by absorbing space from an oversized kitchen. The book-lined area up the steps, once a pantry, contains a television and stereo equipment. Walls are covered in flocked paper with a blue design; cabinets and woodwork are painted blue; and blue beams punctuate the ceiling. Over the blue wall-to-wall carpeting, a small Oriental rug with a red border brings out the red of the wing chair. At the window, draperies in two tones of blue hang from a blue wooden rod.

Three decorative motifs in the kitchen — a vinyl "brick" floor, weathered white paneling, and small geometric pattern — are carried into this family room. The two rooms flow together visually and decoratively. Note that draperies (drawn to the sides of sliding glass doors leading to the deck) repeat in fabric the same geometric pattern of the kitchen and foyer wallpaper. Barn-plank paneling dramatizes walls in both areas. Rusty-orange, used to accent the calm blue and white scheme, is reiterated underfoot in the flooring, in the folding bridge table and chairs, and in the New York Jazz Festival poster over the mantel. Cabinets and shelves flanking the informal brick fireplace include a "wet bar" and provide storage for family room diversions: games, books, a stereo, and a small "wine cellar."

Photos: Yuichi Idaka/Design: Richard Honquest & J. Christopher Jones

Photo: Harry Hartman/Design: J. Allen Scruggs, ASID

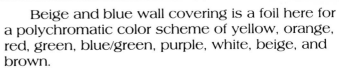

Beige and blue wall covering is a foil here for a polychromatic color scheme of yellow, orange, red, green, blue/green, purple, white, beige, and brown.

Photos: Pedro Guerrero/Design: JoAnn Crews

26

The fantasy of flight is the theme of this comfortable family room. A propeller on a fabric-covered wall echoes the flight motif of a steel gray model plane grouped with photographs on an adjacent wall. Sleek light fixtures on right-angled tracks in the center of the ceiling highlight the collectibles. The carpets are custom-cut to follow the curvilinear line of the sectional seating unit. A mirror under the shelves not only extends the line of the sofa past the architectural limits of the room, but also provides extra light by reflecting or "doubling" a window. On the wall opposite the windows, visually unobtrusive glass shelves display model planes, trophies, a pilot's cap and goggles. The eight patterns used here are compatible because the same colors are used in each.

In this family room, two skylights and track lighting illuminate the dramatic two-story wall embellished with artifacts. They also provide enough light to grow lots of plants.

Photo: Warren Lynch/Design: Patricia Hart McMillan

This den doubles as an elegant dining room. The carpeting is a room-expanding sand tone. Wooden shutters are in keeping with the dark paneling and refined molding. A glass table lightens the effect of the dark room.

Photo: Abrams Photographics/Design: Barbara Winfield

This family room has been designed to capture the mood of a Southwestern desert landscape. A dramatic fireplace wall of native lava rock, illuminated by track lighting, is the room's focal point. The furniture is arranged to divide the room into two areas. The game table and chairs are placed to one side for indoor "competition," while the sofa and two pull-up chairs create a conversation pit in front of the fireplace.

Photos: Everette Short/Design: Ellyn Carol Hirsch

A fireplace and built-in bookcases in this family room serve as a focal point for a conversational grouping of upholstered rattan sofas. The long corridor of thermal glass windows creates a feeling of distance, and increases the sense of space. A cathedral ceiling adds drama. The glass-topped rattan table and the chairs catch the light, airy mood of the outer terrace. A built-in wet bar with a burl-patterned Formica top, mirrored back, and glass shelves is tucked neatly behind louvered pine doors. Nubby draperies contrast with the smooth parquet floor.

eyond this inviting entryway, you can glimpse the family room, which fulfills the foyer's warm promise. Framed 19th-century Comédie Française posters can be seen through the door, as can an ottoman and club chair upholstered in a very contemporary fabric.

Here's a family room for a musically inclined family. The portable school pump organ is still in working order. Above the organ and the sleep sofa, a long shelf provides display space for phonograph records, an Indian tom-tom, Mexican maracas, and other memorabilia. Paneling is the background for an English hunting horn and a debonair straw hat. The dulcimer and cane flute on the coffee table are handmade, as are the floor and sofa cushions. Cushioned-vinyl, no-wax flooring stands up to foot stomping, tap dancing, and daily heavy traffic.

Photo: Hedrich Blessing/Design: Alice Alexander

Photo: Denes Saari/Design: Dayton's Coordinating Staff, Donald O'Donnell, ASID

Cola bottle tops embedded in taping compound stud this family room wall. To do it yourself: Nail lath stripping at edges of the wall. Apply taping compound to the depth of the lath (2 square feet at a time to prevent drying) and push in the bottle tops. A corduroy easy chair and ottoman invite feet-up comfort.

Photo: Vince Lisanti

This luxurious and maintenance-free country retreat is a mélange of pacific monochromatic hues — gray, blue, oatmeal, and sand. All the walls are painted the same slate gray-green of the ceiling. Monotony is avoided because the brick texture of the fireplace wall contrasts with the smoothness of the other walls. Softly shirred casement draperies in a neutral tone reinforce the two subtle patterns, a chevron and a plaid. Warmth is created by a combination of textures: brick, open-weave casement, nubby Herculons, and a flokati area rug. Notice how the choice of hard-edged and slick materials — glass and brass of a coffee table, an end table, and a glass-shelved étagère — act as a perfect foil for the texture and upholstery softness in this contemporary yet rustic setting.

Here is the family room of Pat Boone's house. To meet the expansion of a rapidly growing family, the back porch of the house was converted into a family dining room by extending the area and incorporating a large round dining table. The large light over the table is an old incinerator that was sandblasted and painted. Along the fireplace wall, cushioned seating augments the double sofa arrangement. An area rug adds warmth to this spot by softening the vinyl-covered floor.

Built-in seating/storage cubes mark the entry
to this family room. Carpet-covered cubes and a
built-in banquette give a lot of seating and storage without great expense. To round sharp
edges and to assure greater softness and seating comfort, the cubes (as well as the floor, stairs
from the main floor, base and back of the banquette) were swathed with carpet foundation. In
addition to providing impromptu seating, the
cubes hold a television set, books, and an ampli-
fier. The neutral color scheme is accented with a
vivid wall hanging and throw pillows. Vertical
blinds control natural light; adjustable track lighting gives flexible illumination to every area of the
room.

Design: F. Henry Savage, Jr., ASID

◄ This elegant family room is set up for quiet family activities — putting together a puzzle while sipping wine, knitting, and reading.

▼ The feeling of the Tudor exterior of this house was brought indoors to the family room through the use of massive ceiling beams. The handsome mantel is a beam that was salvaged from a dismantled old barn. Windows are left bare to save expense; since the room looks out on woods, privacy is not a terribly important need. However, to create some privacy, a pair of old barrels are used as tables under the windows to support plants, and other large plants partially shield the room from outside. By floating a large modular pit group in the middle of the room, the need for any more furniture is eliminated. Family portraits in inexpensive brass-toned frames combine with cacti in terra cotta pots to create an "Old West" look.

Photo: Vince Lisanti/Design: Nance Randol

▲ In this brightly colored room, the color scheme is inspired by the myriad hues in the art collection.

Photo: Stan Patz/Design: Angela Nicolaysen

Chapter 2
Basement and Loft Family Rooms

If you're lucky, your house already has a finished basement or attic that you can use as a family room. If not, some paneling, acoustical tile, and resilient flooring can transform unfinished basements and lofts into cozy areas for family lounging. Because no one expects a basement or loft to be as conventionally decorated as the rest of the house, you can give your imagination free rein.

Photo: Darwin Davidson/Design: Evan Frances, ASID, & Sally Alcorn

This basement with small, high windows and little natural light — is a good area for a photographic dark room and film "screenings." Its bright, cheery colors are inspired by those in the vinyl flooring. Because the desk is placed at right angles to the wall, two can use it at the same time. A storage problem is solved by building a pair of tall louvered-doored storage closets into one corner. The projection screen rolls up and out of sight when not in use.

Located in a balcony above the living room, this library-den is a secluded nook for reading and viewing television. The clean-lined uphol-stered sectional combines a sleep sofa, chaise, and ottoman. It blends quietly with the wall — a good visual space-saving trick — and wraps effi-ciently around the corner. Fixtures mounted on the beams provide soft, indirect lighting. The dark beams and railing spark warmth in the cool-colored setting.

Photo: Hans Van Nes Studio/Design: Shirley Regendahl

41

A cozy mood was established in this basement family room with the use of gray barn-plank paneling and a Scottish plaid carpeting. Because it is in the basement and receives the least light of any place in the house, this room was decorated with cheeriness foremost in the mind. Used for watching television, listening to music, reading, or sitting by the wood- and coal-burning stove, the room is also equipped with a billiards table.

Photos: Darwin K. Davidson/Design: Patricia Hart McMillan

In this basement entry foyer is a functional "runway," which goes from the basement door across the family room to a large walk-in closet. Vinyl flooring makes this area an easy-to-maintain place for the family to remove outer garments after skiing and hang them up for drying. There is even a conveniently placed wall phone so if it should ring during the dressing-down process, they can get to it without tracking snow onto the carpet.

This basement room comes alive with vibrant colors. Floor-to-ceiling screens form a wall that can conceal laundry facilities or a furnace.

43

Auxiliary sleeping facilities plus an entertainment center are provided by this "pub" family room. The bar and the stained-glass panels were custom-designed for the far end of the room. In keeping with the English pub theme, darkly stained ceiling beams and diagonal wall beams were applied over white stucco for a Tudor effect. Prints are hung over cross beams to add spots of color, bright foils to the dark woods of the bar and beams. Plaid carpeting establishes the gold, gray, rust, and brown color scheme. The furniture is arranged to divide the room into two conversational areas — one invites chatting around the bar and fireplace on bar stools or club chairs. It is separated from the other area by the love seat and sleep sofa. Next to the sofa is a music and game area.

Photos: John Russell/Design: Betty Smith

When children and grandchildren gather for the holidays, this versatile loft family room is their bailiwick. The sleep sofa becomes a queen-sized bed; two rollaways stashed in the storage room accommodate overflow. The Formica-covered game table is the arena for Scrabble contests. Vertical blinds reinforce the strong architectural character of the sharply angled window wall. The color cue for the room is a series of framed Parisian posters with orange mats.

Photos: Vince Lisanti/Design: Nance Randol Interiors

Design: Margot Gunther, ASID

In this sophisticated basement room, the stark spirit of Southwestern scenery is captured. A sun-bleached palette plays against space expanding white stucco walls, white-painted floor, and white velvet cushions on the built-in sofa. The rest is done with textures and tones: pottery, baskets, subdued blue accents, and the warm brown, suede-look Naugahyde on the lightweight chairs (which fold into the storage cabinet next to the sofa).

Photos: Everette Short/Design: John Mascheroni & J. Christopher Jones

◄ In this loft, a skylight plus a window with bamboo shade make the most of the sun. A decorative assemblage of mirrors hangs above the modular storage units holding a television set and stereo equipment. The sleep sofa, ottomans, and recliner offer comfortable seating. Wood-framed portrait photographs cover the wall in the game corner of the loft. The folding table and chairs are covered in an easy-to-wipe vinyl.

▲ A homemade wall of fake bricks separates this once-sprawling basement into a recreation area and a family "room." The basement's ugly support posts are disguised by boxing them in the brick and adding an arch between the posts. On one side of the homemade wall, the game area has a slate-topped pool table beneath a Tiffany-style lamp; out of sight, a card table provides a place for less strenuous game playing. The family area provides space for family members and their guests to gather on the cotton velvet sectional sofa and relax in clean-lined chrome and leather chairs. Shelves built into one of the arches provide storage. Because the area serves so many purposes, furnishings are carefree and comfortable.

Tin boxes, duck decoys, beer steins, an antique coffee mill, and an old-fashioned telephone warm this cozy, country-style family room. A rustic wood-grain effect throughout is achieved with wall covering — a light tone covers the walls, a darker tone produces the look of wood beams, adding architectural dimension.

Chapter 3
Den-Guest Rooms

If you don't have enough space for a guest bedroom plus a den, you can furnish one room so that it handles both functions. The most important ingredient is a sofa bed that is equally comfortable for lounging and sleeping.

T he tall lamps with oiled-paper parasol shades were made using old goose-necks as a base. The floor cushions were made from an old paisley shawl, the bolsters from a batik fabric. The coffee table is an inexpensive chest covered with fabric, then coated with many layers of red paint. Polyure-thane adds a protective finish.

Design: Benjamin Baldwin

In this sunny den, gray Naugahyde covers the bench below the window. The bench wraps around the wall to become seating for snacking at the fabric-draped table.

P ine paneling acts as a backdrop for a collection of graphics and plates and for the sofa bed in this den. Browns and putty colors are added to the blue and white of the sofa, wall covering, china plates, and vase. French doors open to a sumptuous wood deck with clean-lined, weather-resistant outdoor furniture in beige and brown.

Photos: Yuichi Idaka/Design: Richard Honquest & J. Christopher Jones

Photo: Hans Van Nes/Design: Barbara Egner

ined draperies like those in this den provide privacy, control sunlight, and insulate against cold and heat. The lining protects the fabric from sun, soil, and abrasion and improves the draperies' appearance. The built-in couch has a shelf behind it that holds drinks and plants. Since the fabric is busy, the furnishings are kept simple.

Desert colors dominate this Indian-accented den. Pastel tones of tan, gold, rust, and turquoise provide an appealing background for the clean lines of the furnishings.

A collection of natural materials — wicker and pottery — key the earth tones in this rustic den. The theme continues with raffia floor matting, a grouping of framed prints and mirrors, and washable vinyl grass cloth in a terra cotta color on the walls and in straw color on cabinet fronts and backs of bookshelves.

Photo: Keith Morton/Design: Patricia Gaylor

Converting a bedroom to this guest room-den was simple, since the room was originally furnished with just such a future in mind. The brass-skirted lighting fixture, Scandinavian rosewood furniture, sleep sofa, and Portuguese area rug are all holdovers from the original girl's bedroom. The built-in, Formica-topped storage cabinet beneath the windows serves as a bar during large parties and holds a collection of musical instruments. The inlaid Moroccan chest is new, as are the vinyl pedestal chairs.

Design: Evelyn Kittay

Photos: Everette Short/Design: Audrey Brown Bender

Beige cowhide adds warmth to the parquet floor in this den. Treasures are gathered from all over the world: the guitar rests near a wood Japanese chest, painted in traditional Oriental red and black hues. The classic Eames chair is bent plywood and leather. Floor cushions are hand-woven African fabric. The fabric collage is dyed canvas cut or torn into free shapes and then mounted on canvas. A pair of old picnic baskets now hold magazines.

The casement windows in this den were removed to make room for window greenhouses, which are attached to a frame on the outside of the house. They are a perfect covering for the twin windows at the south end of this long, narrow room. Visually, the rows of plants widen the room. The greenhouse effect is continued with hanging plants at the other windows.

Photo: Alan Hicks

During the day, sunlight filters through bamboo blinds in this den. At night and on oppressively hot days, the wood-paneled shutters are closed for extra protection against the heat. The queen-sized sofa bed in a cotton, wood-grain print has fold-over cushion arms and knife-edged pillows.

Photo: Photographic House/Design: Ron Bundy, ASID

◄ Paneling, chosen for its country look, was installed horizontally in this den-music room/guest bedroom. The spectacular light fixture is made of Oriental paper shades and two, four-foot fluorescent tubes. The antique wicker chair, table, and pictures are perfectly at home with the contemporary pillows and Finnish wall hanging, which has been appliquéd and stuffed for a trapunto look.

Photo: Vince Lisanti/Design: Jerry Gonzalez

Simplicity is the key to this den. The sleeper sofa is surrounded by light-box cubes. An overhead bridge visually enlarges the room, frames the window, and adds spot lighting. Additional storage and seating are arranged along the wall. One small cube serves as a coffee table.

The sofa, covered in beige cut velvet, and the richly patterned leaf wall covering, impart a timeless quality to this den. Coordinating fabric covers the pads on the platform, which are made from 1/2-inch plywood. Six feet of carpet creates an area rug that goes right up and over the platform. The bright blue color is continued up the wall with matching paint. Framed florals are cutouts from scraps of wall covering, reassembled on blue construction paper to form bouquets. Dime store frames with brown wrapping paper borders complete the clever artwork. Woven placemats, glued to the top of the cube table and set between the platform pads, add texture.

Upholstered modular seating in rust cotton duck, and interlocking storage cubes that form a cocktail table, create an uncluttered effect in this den. The channel-quilted love seat and chair unfold to provide sleeping accommodations for up to three guests. The clever furniture arrangement forms a niche for the drop-leaf wall unit that serves as a desk. Note the use of the windowsill to hold photographs, furthering the niche illusion. The low end table/magazine rack is actually a bed tray, and it makes lap dining or doing crossword puzzles very convenient. A Chinese wedding basket is a handy portable carrier for sewing or needlework. A swivel scissor lamp is placed to allow light to shine at the desk or sofa. The deeply sculptured area rug adds texture and a touch of luxury.

Photo: Ernest Silva/Design: Michael Cannarozzi

➤ A lambrequin and matchstick bamboo blinds frame the large window in this den. The lambrequin's natural-tone fabric — an exact match to the covering on the sofa — makes the window melt unobtrusively into the wall. Serving the sleep sofa by day is a hammered-brass table. The wall paneling is made of pine planks.

Photographic House/Design: Ron Bundy, ASID

Design: Evelyn Kittay

◄ The right-angled placement of this sofa and love seat creates a conversational grouping and allows the television to be viewed across the room. Note the placement of the relaxing chair with ottoman; it is deliberately isolated from the conversational grouping and near the bookshelves for someone who prefers reading to television.

Photo: Denes Saari/Design: Dayton's Coordinating Staff, Donald O'Donnell, ASID

In this duck hunter's den, twin plaid-covered sofas and a tweedy club chair go with the rustic pine furnishings. The lath-striped walls are made by nailing lath stripping at eight-inch intervals, filling between strips with taping compound, and using a notched trowel to texture the surface.

A modular seating unit provides comfortable lounging and television viewing in this den. There's no need for a single lamp here — track lighting does it all. The television is topped with a painted fabric hanging and accented with a red planter. Against the paneling, a painting is framed in the green of the painted walls opposite.

Photo: Everette Short/Design: Evan Frances, ASID, & J. Christopher Jones

The artworks on the wall of this den are photographs clipped from a glossy calendar. Versatile modular seating pieces supply comfortable lounging and sleeping, and can be easily rearranged. The "molding" that runs around the door along the baseboard is made of masking tape. An ordinary matchstick window blind is embroidered with a giant cross-stitch in colors to echo the print on the seating pieces. The throw pillows pick up the background colors in the pictures.

Photo: Ernie Silva Studio/Design: Michael Cannarozzi

Lightweight, easily moved furniture is the main feature of this den. The sofa, which doubles as a bed, is made by placing foam pads on a build-it-yourself platform of 3/4-inch plywood. A durable fabric is used to insure its long-time wear. Two lawn chairs are painted to match the wall and are cushioned for indoor comfort. White painted branches are used to make a spidery wall sculpture that bridges the two windows. A bright area rug defines the conversation area.

71

Photo: Darwin Davidson/Design: Evan Frances, ASID & Sally Alcorn

Chapter 4
Garden Rooms

You can create a sun-filled den by enclosing your patio, breezeway, or porch. Add wicker furnishings and lots of plants, and your den will have a garden ambience year-round.

This garden room was created from a screened-in breezeway that connected the house to the garage. On the street side of the house, screening was replaced with siding to match the exterior for a more permanent look. At the rear, screening was replaced with glass sliding doors. Existing slate floors and exposed rafters add to the garden-room effect. An intimate seating grouping at the far end of the room takes advantage of a niche created by the jutting garage wall. A lattice screen and table accentuate the garden mood.

Photo: Keith Morton/Design: Patricia Gaylor

Decorate with white; that's the message in this sun-filled garden room. White furnishings and accessories will show off indoor potted plants to their best advantage. A trio of white butterflies on the display wall drift above white shelves and a white wicker-look oval mirror. More white is used in the framed prints in the seating area. The trellis-pattern wall covering and drapery fabric complete the outdoors mood.

L arge terra cotta Mexican tiles warm the foyer and sunroom floors here. White wicker and a profusion of greenery create the garden-room ambience. Lots of sunlight streams in through the stained glass.

Photo: Richard Champion/Design: Carleton Varney

S ince this trellised patio is used year-round, a careful balance is achieved between the moods of winter and summer. Thus, the warmth of terra cotta-painted walls and ceiling is overlaid with the cool look of white trellis. A woodsy, green fern upholstery print acts as an extension of the garden beyond. To make the trellised room cozy in winter, the living room fireplace was opened up and extended out to the patio. Rather than replace the old patio furniture, it was painted white and covered with printed upholstery. For practicality underfoot, sisal squares are used; individual squares that are badly worn or stained can be lifted out and replaced.

Photo: Ernie Silva Studio/Design: Margot Gunther

➤ Because this corner in the back of a little house is tight and somewhat dark, a yellow color scheme was chosen to bring sunshine indoors. And because the scheme is monochromatic, it expands the room visually; the upholstery fabrics blend with the bright yellow walls, which also makes the room seem larger. The choice of circular see-through glass tables helps the room-expanding effect. Brass highlights bounce light through the room, adding even more sparkle.

➤ The dark paneling and sisal floor covering here give a rustic effect. The white table and delicate floral print keep the room looking light and airy in spite of the heavy effect of the walls.

Sleeping facilities for one guest are provided in this den by the window seat, which has an artichoke motif stenciled on its draperies and trapunto pillows. The shirred wall covering is unbleached muslin dribbled with dye, the same technique used on the round tablecloth. Bamboo blinds over the window and the basket on the table provide texture.

An old-fashioned, many-windowed porch can be turned into a garden room like this one, where you can bask in the sunshine and tend your plants. White makes a sparkling background for a room where the sun streams in all day. Using a one-color scheme is a wonderful unifier too, which is important to remember when the furnishings are comprised of many small pieces. Because there's plenty of natural pattern in the leaves, branches, and fern fronds, it makes good decorating sense to stick to just one fabric print. On the floor is a grass-green indoor/outdoor carpet. The windows are covered in macramé panels made from common clothesline.

Photos: John Russell/Design: Betty Smith

I n this airy family room adjoining a greenhouse, cane, rattan, light elm furnishings, and
a rush rug are natural foils for the greenery
visible through the glass door. Sunlight pours
in through the thin-slat blinds. The blinds and rattan screen play pattern on pattern with the Chinese grass rug. A rattan table and chairs create a
quiet corner for two.

Chapter 5
Dens for Hobbies and Offices

In many homes, the den doubles as an office or an area to pursue a favorite hobby. With a little imagination and the proper furnishings, you can turn your den into a library, music room, sewing room, or even an exercise room.

Bold, horizontally striped fabric on the walls of this tiny den-sewing room visually enlarge the space. The sewing table, supported at either end by bookcases, can be removed 'to give access to the utility area behind it.

For people who want to spend more time with their children but need to put in nights and weekends at the office, here is a combination family room/home office. To create an office-away-from-the-office, a Formica-clad Parsons table was placed behind a sofa to serve as a desk. A file cabinet in a closet (not shown) holds necessary papers. Besides creating an efficient work space, this placement offers a view of the glowing fire and a view out the window into the garden. All the furnishings, wall coverings, and carpeting are child-proof — easily cleaned and stain resistant. An oversized armoire holds a television set and also stores books and games. Note how this one out-of-scale piece makes the room seem taller and wider. The boxed-in crown molding hiding the drapery rod also adds height.

Photo: Hedrich-Blessing/Design: Montgomery Ward Home Furnishings Staff

This den serves as an office reception area for a business executive, but on weekends it's the family den. Residential furnishings prevent the room from becoming just a waiting room and make it cozy enough for family lounging and accommodating guests. The sofa opens into a bed, and the window seat holds pillows, blankets, and linens. The recliner is perfect for end-of-day relaxation.

Photo: Abrams Photographics/Design: Barbara Winfield

This library-music room agreeably combines a camelback Chippendale love seat, fan-back Windsor chair, and Sheraton side chair.

A cozy space to sit by the fire and a place to serve as a home office are provided in this small room. A closet to the right of the fireplace was subdivided into three sections for convenient storage. The bottom section holds logs for the fireplace. The desk, a glass-topped rattan piece, was placed next to the window to provide a well-lighted work surface.

The carpeting in this den is burnt orange, complementing the wood tones in the walnut desk, cube table, and shelves, and the two rich brown prints on the window shade and sleep sofa. The chair and ottoman are covered in a third print compatible with the overall beige scheme.

Photo: Hedrich-Blessing/Design: Montgomery Ward Home Furnishings Staff

In this raised library corner, an old brick wall melds handsomely with the bookcases, a slant-top pine desk, and a woven wood shade.

An upstairs den was turned into this exercise room, complete with bicycle, rowing machine, jump rope, and other paraphernalia. The wire basket cart, shelf units, and clothes hooks collect miscellaneous sports equipment and towels. Larger items are stored "aloft" on a built-in storage rack. Mirror panels visually expand the room. The lush carpeting softens the floor and unifies this area with an adjoining bedroom.

Photo: Bill Hedrich/Design: Patricia Laughman & J. Christopher Jones

Bookcases were extended to the ceiling in this den to make it useful as a library. The green wall-to-wall carpeting creates a sophisticated look.

Photos: Carl K. Shuman/Design: Thomas Hills Cook

Design: Peg Walker

◄   In this porch enclosure, sunny yellow cloth window shades have fabric loops that hold painted rod pulls.

Parquet was placed on this battered office desk that's topped with a hollow-core door. It gives the desk an executive look, at a low cost.

Here, a conversation pit/electronic music room is designed around an oak-stained curio cabinet. The cabinet is built around an octagonal opening in the floor with a view of the living room below. The raised floor covered in carpeting conceals deep storage bunkers; additional storage is built in behind the backs of seating.

Photos: Everette Short/Design: Evan Frances, ASID

Photo: Photographic House/Design: G. Allen Scruggs

An insulated attic was converted into this weaving and sewing room by enlarging one window to provide ample light for the weaver. A dramatically colored, no-wax vinyl flooring covers the floor. Brightly painted industrial shelving holds baskets of yarns, pattern books, and other materials. A Parsons table in the foreground, painted the same bright color as the shelves, serves as a desk and sewing center. Beams and moldings, fitted with spindles to hold skeins of yard, add a decorative note.

When this porch was expanded, refurbishing was done in the Mediterranean style of the house. Thin-slat venetian blinds at the windows screen out glare and help with climate control. The international style of the decoration is inspired by the Moorish-style architecture. This feeling is enhanced by the use of a brass coffee table, piles of floor pillows, and a large Oriental rug. Open-weave rattan furniture and potted plants add to the faraway feeling of this retreat.

An unused closet divides neatly into a built-in bar and seating alcove. The rear wall is swathed in blue sheeting, and the seating alcove is curtained to match. The bench cushion in matching fabric is in tawny beige. A red cushion and curtain tie-backs complete the three-color scheme. Gold-toned accents add a touch of glitter.

Photo: Ernest Silva/Design: Penni Paul

▼   This handsome family room incorporates space for three hobbies — the collecting of good books, wines, and photographs of family and friends. All three hobbies were considered in the initial design concept for floor-to-ceiling, wall-to-wall shelving that wraps around the room, utilizing what otherwise would be wasted space. Simple but elegantly constructed wine storage is provided by the tall rack that is actually part of a refreshment center, complete with base cabinet storage, a counter top for serving, and a sink. A display space for portraits occupies the major part of one wall. The photographs serve as a dominant decorating element, bringing a sense of life and movement into this rather quiet setting. Beneath the portrait gallery, a cantilevered shelf fills the need for a desk and library table. The bookshelves are asymmetrically designed, which contributes to the informal feeling.

Photo: Milt Techner

Photo: Everette Short/Design: Ellen Frankel & J. Christopher Jones

This music room-den, where an antique organ vies for attention with the newest stereo equipment, is an intimate space to put up your feet and relax. To strengthen the acoustical balance in the room, a deep blue oval carpet has been placed over the tile floor. The comfortable love seat and wing chair with ottoman encourage informal lounging.

➤ This bedroom converted to an office has residential furniture that serves the owner's professional needs, yet blends with the design of the rest of the house. Desert colors, Southwestern-style patterns and textures in the area rugs, pillows, bowls, baskets, and plants are used to evoke the desert landscape.

If your hobby is sitting near a cozy fire and reading, this is the den for you. A wall was torn down between this room and a former kitchen to create one large space. Brick covers the wall behind the floor and beneath a cast-iron stove. Prefinished, easily maintained hardwood parquet flooring grows more beautiful as it ages. On the walls, oak paneling complements the no-drip acrylic paint.

Photo: Alan Hicks/Design: Russ English & Mark Perry

Photo: Abrams Photographics/Design: Barbara Winfield